THE
1950s

Richard Tames

Franklin Watts
London · New York · Toronto · Sydney

Franklin Watts Inc.
387 Park Avenue South
New York, N.Y. 10016

Library of Congress Cataloging-in-Publication Data

Tames, Richard
    The 1950s/Richard Tames.
        p.   cm.—(The Picture history of the 20th century)
    Bibliography: p.
    Includes index.
    Summary: Text and pictures highlight the main events of the 1950s.
    ISBN 0–531–14034–2
    1. History, Modern—1945—Pictorial works—Juvenile literature.
    [1. History, Modern—1945–]   I. Title.   II. Series.
    D842.5.T36   1989
    909.82′5—dc20   88–50367
                                              CIP
                                              AC

Design: K and Co
Editor: Hazel Poole
Picture Research: Jan Croot, Sarah Ridley
Printed in Belgium

Photographs: Associated Press 16(C), 17(B), 34(B); Norman Barrett 39(TL); British Airways 41(TL); J. Allen Cash Photolibrary 25(CL); Cinerama 32(T); Jan Croot 28(R), 31(C), 31(B), 41(TR); Daily Mirror 15(B); Horace Dobbs 21(TL); with gratitude to the EMI Music Archives 29(TR); Hulton-Deutsch 7(B), 9(B), 12(B), 16(T), 19(BL), 19(BR), 22(BR), 23(B), 30(T), 30(BL), 31(TL), 34(T), 36(T), 37(B), 39(TR), 39(BL), 41(C), 42(BR); Kobal Collection 29(B), 30(BR), 32(B), 33(T), 33(BL), 33(BR); Kontiki Museum, Oslo 21(TR); Museum of London 23(T), 23(C); New York Picture Collection 41(B), Novosti 19(TR); Popperfoto 6(T), 7(T), 15(T), 15(C), 18(B), 20(BL), 21(B), 22(T), 22(BL), 25(CL), 25(CR), 26(BL), 27(TL), 27(TR), 27(C), 27(B), 29(C), 35(TL), 35(TR), 36(B), 37(TL), 38(T), 38(B), 40(T), 40(B); Retrograph Archive Collection 28(BL); Science Photo Library 42(T), 43(T), 43(CL); Cecil Beaton photograph courtesy of Sotheby's London 26(BR); Tass 9(T); Topham 6(CR), 6(B), 8(T), 8(B), 9(C), 10(B), 11(TL), 11(TR), 11(B), 12(T), 13(T), 13(BL), 13(BR), 14(T), 14(B), 16(B), 17(TL), 17(TR), 20(T), 39(BR), 42(BL), 43(B); UPI/Bettmann Newsphoto 19(TL), 35(B), 37(TR); UK Atomic Energy Authority 18(BR); Basil Spence Partnership/Mead Gallery, Warwick University 25(TL); ZEFA 24(BL), 24(BR), 25(BL). (Map on p. 10 by Stan Johnson).

cover: Kobal Collection/Popperfoto
frontispiece: Popperfoto

Contents

Introduction

The 1940s had seen most of the world's peoples gripped in the agony of war. The 1950s brought peace to most and a new prosperity to many. The United States emerged as the world's pre-eminent power, its forces scattered on military bases around the globe, its population enjoying a standard of living previously unknown to any nation in history and envied throughout the world. American prestige and self-confidence were blighted, however, by racial injustice and the fear of communism, both at home and abroad. Beside Soviet Russia arose a mighty new ally, a communist China, though their alliance was not to outlast the decade.

Britain hailed a new era with the coronation of a new Queen but, like France, struggled with colonial problems while their former enemies, Germany and Japan, astonished them with their vitality in rebuilding shattered economies. The creation of closer ties between the countries of western Europe promised well for the future but over all humankind was cast the shadow of the nuclear bomb.

In its impact on everyday life, however, the effect of ever-advancing technology was no less imposing. Television, cheap electrical appliances and mass-produced cars transformed the life-styles and leisure of millions, though these changes were largely confined to the Western world. The peoples of Asia and Africa benefitted from more basic improvements in health and diet which helped to fuel a "population explosion" which was, in turn, to create new pressures for migration, urban growth and environmental damage. As the decade closed, the atomic age merged with the space age as satellite photographs showed more dramatically than ever before that today the world was one, however much its peoples were still divided and in conflict.

The United States in the 1950s

International events in the closing years of the 1940s set the stage for the strange mixture of apprehension and self confidence that marked the new decade. In 1949, the Soviet Union had detonated its first atomic bomb, and the following year the United States found itself plunged into a war in Korea.

When the Korean War ended in 1953, having cost 33,629 American lives (and at least 200 times as many Korean ones), American troops remained behind to guard the peace, as they did in Germany. The fall of Senator Joseph McCarthy and the death of Joseph Stalin seemed to promise a thaw in the "cold war," but the Soviet invasion of Hungary and the launching of *Sputnik I* were harsh reminders of a continuing challenge.

The Montgomery bus boycott in 1955 and the court-ordered desegregation of the Little Rock public schools in 1957 heralded the beginning of the civil rights movement under the leadership of the Rev. Martin Luther King, Jr., and foreshadowed the coming social changes.

Despite all, the U.S. economy remained robust, and Americans continued to demonstrate their belief in the future through an unprecedented "baby boom."

IMMEDIATE RELEASE   APRIL 10, 1951

ORDER TO GENERAL MacARTHUR FROM THE PRESIDENT

I deeply regret that it becomes my duty as President and Commander in Chief of the United States military forces to replace you as Supreme Commander, Allied Powers; Commander in Chief, United Nations Command; Commander in Chief, Far East; and Commanding General, U. S. Army, Far East.

You will turn over your commands, effective at once, to Lt. Gen. Matthew B. Ridgway. You are authorized to have issued such orders as are necessary to complete desired travel to such place as you select.

My reasons for your replacement will be made public concurrently with the delivery to you of the foregoing order, and are contained in the next following message. (See attached Statement by the President.)

△ United Nations' troops went to the aid of South Korea after they were invaded by North Korea in 1950. When the Korean War ended in 1953, there was still intense bitterness between North and South.

△ In April 1951, President Truman dismissed MacArthur from command for failure to stop making conflicting political remarks.

◁ Senator Joseph McCarthy grins at an advertisement denouncing his "crusade" against alleged communists. His smears and bullying tactics ruined many lives before his attack on the army brought him down.

▷ The evangelist Billy Graham became the most outstanding crusader for popular Christianity on both sides of the Atlantic. Graham, seen here addressing a crowd of 40,000 from the steps of Washington's Capitol building, showed that the power of personality in direct confrontation with a live audience could still count for much.

▽ In September 1957, President Eisenhower compelled the enforcement of a Supreme Court ruling against racial segregation in education by ordering 1,000 paratroopers to guard nine black children who wished to attend the Central High School in Little Rock, Arkansas.

The communist world

By 1950, Russian-backed Communist parties had seized power throughout eastern Europe. The wartime "Grand Alliance" would be replaced by two armed camps – the North Atlantic Treaty Organization (NATO) and the Russian-dominated Warsaw Pact. Distrust was fueled by mutual espionage and rivalry in developing atomic weapons and spacecraft, but the violent confrontations of this "cold war" era took place outside divided Europe. In 1950, Korea, "temporarily" divided since 1945, saw the Communist government of the north try to reunify the country by force. The weak south turned to the United States for help. Aided by over a dozen allies, the United States, under a United Nations flag, finally stabilized the continued division of the country along the 38th parallel after three years of bloody fighting. Stalin's death in 1953 led to the secret trial and execution of his police chief, Beria, and the rise of Nikita Khrushchev as first secretary of the Communist Party. Khrushchev denounced Stalin's persecutions and proclaimed the hope of "peaceful coexistence" with the West but still crushed popular risings in Poland and Hungary. China, meanwhile, went its own way in adapting communism to its needs.

▽ Chinese troops crossing a river during their 1950 invasion of Tibet. A revolt in 1958 cost 65,000 Tibetan lives and forced the Dalai Lama, Tibet's spiritual leader, into exile in India.

△ Bewildered civilians in Pyongyang, capital of North Korea, after its capture by American troops in October 1950. The Chinese took it back in December but lost it again in June 1951.

◁ Muscovites read Pravda's black-bordered confirmation of Stalin's death in March 1953 after nearly thirty years of dictatorial rule. The full scale of his tyranny took another thirty years to be revealed.

▽ In November 1956, the Soviet Union sent tanks into Hungary to crush a national rising against its domination. 20,000 people died and 200,000 fled to the West as Russian control was reasserted.

▽ In July 1959, Vice-President Richard M. Nixon, visiting Moscow, receives a playful gesture of peace from Soviet Premier Khrushchev at an American exhibition. In a mock-up of a gadget-filled American kitchen, the two then argued heatedly for an hour about the rival merits of capitalism and communism.

Europe

By the 1950s, the scars of war were healing in western Europe. Devastated West Germany made an "economic miracle" out of hard work, while Italy showed its old flair in films, fashion and design. Spain, still wretchedly poor, began to benefit from tourism. France, however, suffered from a succession of weak governments and colonial wars. Persistent efforts were made for closer cooperation, though ambitious plans for a "United States of Europe" failed. In 1951 Belgium, the Netherlands and Luxembourg (already joined as Benelux, a customs union) linked with France, Germany and Italy to form the European Coal and Steel Community, which formed the basis for the European Economic Community, set up by the Treaty of Rome in 1957. The Nordic Council of Scandinavian states was another example of practical cooperation.

▽ **Signing the Allied-West German Peace Contract 1952. (Left to right) Eden, Schuman, Acheson and Adenauer.**

▷ **EFTA, the European Free Trade Association was set up in 1959 to rival the "Common Market."**

▨	European Free Trade Association
▨	European Economic Community
☐	Western Europe

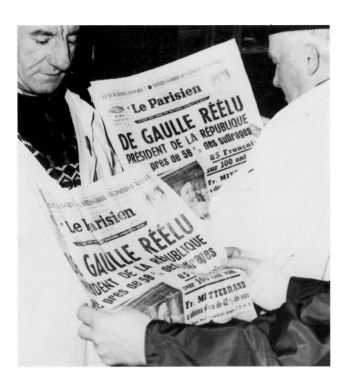

△ De Gaulle's 1958 landslide victory enabled him to begin the tricky task of French withdrawal from Algeria.

▷ General Charles de Gaulle emerged from retirement to lead France in response to Algeria's crisis.

▷ U.S. garrison troops parade through the streets of Frankfurt in an "Army Day" march. In 1955 a partially rearmed West Germany was admitted to the NATO alliance but it was clear to most Germans that American forces were still needed to guarantee security against the Soviet threat.

Leaders rise and fall

Throughout Asia and Africa, the new politics of independence exacted a high price from its leaders. Assassins killed King Abdullah of Jordan and Prime Minister Liaquat Ali Khan of Pakistan in 1951, King Faisal of Iraq in 1958 and Prime Minister Bandaranaike of Sri Lanka in 1959. Luxury-loving King Farouk of Egypt was lucky to flee to comfortable exile after the 1952 army coup, as was Argentine dictator Juan Peron who unwisely threatened the authority of the Catholic Church.

But others showed remarkable staying power. Bourguiba of Tunisia achieved independence for his country in 1956 and was to stay its leader for thirty years. Lee Kuan Yew of Singapore was to do the same after becoming Prime Minister in 1959. Other major newcomers were Dr. Verwoerd, chief architect of South Africa's apartheid policies, and visionary Kwame Nkrumah who led the wealthy Gold Coast to independence as Ghana in 1957, then drove it to near-bankruptcy. The best-loved world figure of the decade was undoubtedly Cardinal Roncalli who became Pope John XXIII in 1958.

△ The immense funeral cortege of Eva Peron in Buenos Aires. Ex-film star Evita used glamour and corruption to build her personal power.

▽ Hussein Ibn Talal leaves Amman's main mosque after being crowned King of Jordan on his 18th birthday. He is surrounded by Bedouin troops of the famed Arab legion, on whose personal loyalty his rule depended. He survived many assassination attempts, pursuing a pro-Western policy.

Scenting victory – Cypriot leader Archbishop Makarios (top) is hailed at Athens airport in 1959. Dr. Hastings Banda (left) was imprisoned by the British in 1959 but later led Malawi to independence. Fidel Castro (below) takes the oath of office as Cuba's youngest-ever Prime Minister in 1959 after his guerrillas overthrow dictator Batista.

Suez

In 1952, King Farouk of Egypt was overthrown by a "Free Officers" movement in the army. They wanted to end ties with Britain, who regarded control of the Suez Canal as vital for the defense of her worldwide empire and trade. In 1954, an Anglo-Egyptian treaty withdrew British troops from the Canal Zone but the British and French governments kept control of the Suez Canal Company which ran the international waterway. When Western powers refused to aid Egypt in building its Aswan Dam project, Free Officers' leader Colonel Nasser took over the Canal Company in July 1956 to use its profits to pay for the dam. Both sides saw the issue as a matter of national pride and repeated negotiations failed to find a compromise on the future of the canal. Britain and France prepared for war, secretly agreeing that Israel should attack Egypt, so that they could claim to be separating the two sides in the interests of peaceful users of the canal. On October 29, Israel invaded the Sinai peninsula. An Anglo-French invasion on November 5 was called off under pressure from the United States. Nasser's success led Syria to join Egypt to form the United Arab Republic.

▷ Israeli troops gather to attack Egyptian outposts in Sinai. The peninsula was to remain in Israeli hands until a negotiated withdrawal in 1982.

◁ All smiles in 1955 as Eden, Britain's Foreign Secretary, visits Cairo. But Eden privately considered Nasser a dictator to be met by force if necessary.

(Below opposite) Crowds in Alexandria applaud Nasser's announcement of the Suez Canal takeover. The failed Anglo-French invasion made him a hero.

△ Troops of a United Nations emergency peace-keeping force arrive as British paratroopers depart. The United Nations provided a forum for international denunciation of Britain and France.

ISRAEL'S SHIPS BARRED BY EGYPT FOR 7 YEARS

◁ British cartoonist Vicky satirizes Eden as a latter-day Admiral Nelson, deliberately ignoring obvious dangers to pursue his own plans. Unlike Nelson, Eden found that stubbornness and misjudgment were to cost him his career. He resigned as Prime Minister in January 1957.

"THE CANAL MUST BE RUN EFFICIENTLY AND KEPT OPEN, AS IT HAS ALWAYS BEEN IN THE PAST, AS A FREE AND INTERNATIONAL WATERWAY FOR THE SHIPS OF ALL NATIONS"
—SIR ANTHONY EDEN

15

Ending empires

The former greatness of the European powers rested in part on their possession of overseas empires. Whatever their economic value, which was often questionable, they conferred political prestige and diplomatic leverage. Exhausted as a result of World War II, however, Europe increasingly lacked both the will and the means to resist colonial demands for the rights that Europeans themselves enjoyed in terms of self-government.

Both the French and the Dutch fought vainly to reassert their power by force. Britain finally accepted the inevitable once it had decided to part with India in 1947. In Malaya, however, British troops fought skillfully and successfully to defeat a Communist rebellion before handing over power in 1957.

△ "Mau Mau" suspects in a Kenyan prison camp. This rural rebellion, part tribal war, part conflict for land, cost 235 European and 13,000 African lives between 1952 and 1960.

△ In April 1955 representatives of 29 African and Asian states met at Bandung in Indonesia in an attempt to distance themselves from the "cold war" confrontations of the superpowers.

▷ The Duchess of Kent dances with Kwame Nkrumah at a ball to mark Ghanaian independence—a symbol of British willingness to end colonial rule without prolonged bloodshed.

◁ Tunisia's Habib Bourguiba (1903–) managed to achieve a peaceful disengagement from French rule in 1956 but kept his country on economically beneficial terms with the former imperial power.

△ French paratroopers counterattacking a Viet Minh site. The long French effort to reassert control over Indo-China ended in defeat at Dien Bien Phu, a French trap in which the French were themselves entrapped.

◁ The struggle for Algerian independence from France led to terror and torture on both sides. Here French troops round up suspected "rebel sympathizers." The French army remained unbeaten but the war so divided France that it lost the will to hold on.

The atomic age

In 1950 the United States began research to make a "super bomb," more powerful than the one that had wiped out Hiroshima in 1945. In November 1952 an experimental "device" vaporized Eniwetok Atoll in the Marshall Islands of the Pacific into a mushroom cloud of dust 40 km (25 miles) high and 161 km (100 miles) across and in 1953, Russia tested an actual bomb. By 1955, both Russia and the United States were already at least willing to talk about nuclear disarmament as eminent scientists issued the "Pugwash manifesto," calling for a halt to the atomic arms race. By 1957 Britain, too, had its own "H-bomb." That year Britain's "White Paper on Defense" admitted ". . . There is at present no means of providing adequate protection for the people of this country against nuclear attack." The most people could hope for was a four minute warning of the approach of missiles. In 1958, Nobel prize-winner Linus Pauling presented the United Nations with the signatures of 9,000 scientists, stressing the genetic danger from even testing nuclear weapons and calling for their ending. This was supported by mass protests in both the United States and Britain. But the cost of the arms race was probably more decisive in leading to the 1963 partial "test ban treaty," long after both sides had stockpiled enough bombs to achieve "Mutually Assured Destruction"—MAD.

◁ Troops of the Eleventh U.S. Airborne Division watch an A-bomb test outside Las Vegas, Nevada as part of a combined maneuvers exercise. As time passed, it became clear that even such limited exposure could drastically increase the risks of developing cancer.

▽ Queen Elizabeth II opening Britain's first atomic power station at Calder Hall in 1956. In 1955 the government announced its plans to build 12 nuclear plants over the next 10 years.

◁ Americans knew that millions of Britons had survived Hitler's blitz thanks to deep concrete bunkers. Some, therefore, put their faith in model "fall-out shelters" to protect them from the effects of a nuclear holocaust.

△ The Soviet Union's nuclear-powered ice-breaker *Lenin* showed the practical uses of the atom. In 1957 the U.S. nuclear submarine, *Nautilus*, sailed under the North Pole, opening a new dimension in secret warfare.

▷ In February 1950, Dr. Klaus Fuchs, a German-born Communist working in British atomic research was charged with giving secret data to the Soviet Union following an FBI tip-off. He may have saved the Soviets an estimated ten years of research and this fear hastened the Western commitment to make an "H-bomb" to keep ahead of Russia. Sentenced to 14 years in prison and deprived of his British citizenship, Fuchs was freed in 1959 and deported to East Germany. Fuchs's interrogation led eventually to the denunciation of Ethel and Julius Rosenberg as atom spies in the United States. They were sentenced to death. Protesting their innocence, they went to the electric chair in June 1953.

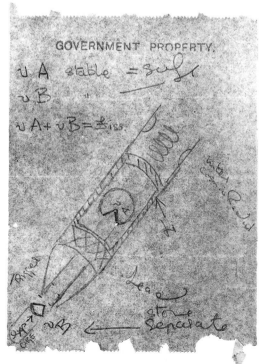

Exploration and adventure

By the mid-twentieth century, few regions of the world's surface remained undiscovered but the challenge to penetrate its heights and depths remained and increasingly relied on advances in science and technology. The conquest of Everest, for example, depended on the meticulous observation of weather conditions by expedition leader John Hunt and the use of such hi-tech novelties as high altitude nylon clothing and light-weight oxygen equipment.

Exploration was becoming essentially a team effort and one determined as much by the funds and initiatives of government as by the courage and daring of individuals. 1958 saw both American and New Zealand scientific teams at the South Pole, while a British expedition under Dr. Vivian Fuchs made the first overland crossing of the Antarctic.

In 1959, a further hopeful sign for the future was a twelve-nation agreement on a draft treaty to keep the whole Antarctic region as a demilitarized scientific reserve, open to all nations and free from pressures for commercial development. And if science and the systematic approach threatened to take the romance out of exploration, film and television now enabled distant millions to see it happen before their own eyes.

△ New Zealander Edmund Hillary photographed by Nepali sherpa Tenzing Norgay at the summit of Mount Everest, 29,002 feet above sea-level, on May 29, 1953. News of their triumph reached Britain on the morning of Queen Elizabeth II's coronation.

◁ An ice-pick marks the relative size of the alleged "footprint" of a yeti. This 1951 photo was followed by unconfirmed sightings of the Himalayas' legendary "Abominable Snowman" by later expeditions.

△ Norwegian Thor Heyerdahl's "Kontiki" expedition saw a six-man crew sail a balsa wood raft 6,400 kilometers (4,000 miles) to show that Polynesians might have come from South America originally by sea.

△ Diver wearing an aqualung, invented by the French explorer Commander Jacques Cousteau. He developed underwater television techniques from his ship *Calypso* to reveal the underwater world of sea-bed life in his 1956 film *The Silent World.*

▷ *U.S.S. Glacier* plows through the Ross Sea as part of "Operation Deep Freeze," a cooperative American—New Zealand scientific investigation of conditions in the Antarctic.

Uncovering the past

1952 was an epoch-making year for the understanding of the remote past. Young Michael Ventris cracked the secret of Linear B, the ancient script which had puzzled generations of scholars, and in the same year the invention of radiocarbon dating gave archaeologists a revolutionary new method of accurately estimating the age of once-living materials, like wood or cloth, for as far back as 4,500 years. The year closed with the discovery by scientists in South Africa of the coelacanth, a species of fish thought to have been extinct for over 40,000,000 years.

Archaeology continued to grab the headlines throughout the decade. In 1953, W. Le Gros Clark demonstrated conclusively that the so-called Piltdown man – Eoanthropus dawsonii – was nothing but an elaborate hoax that had fooled the experts for over forty years by combining a human skull and an ape jaw to produce a 'missing link' in the evolutionary chain. Important excavations of the 1950s dealt with Nonsuch Palace, Elizabeth I's favored retreat, and the 'Vasa', a remarkably preserved 17th-century Swedish warship.

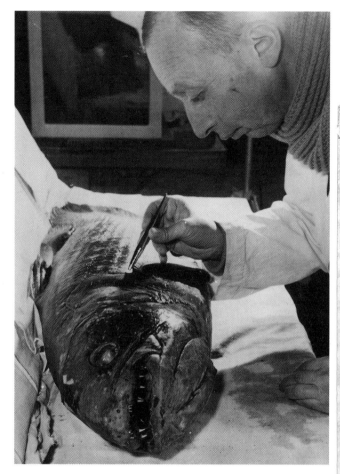

△ Examining one of three coelacanth caught off Madagascar.

◁ The head of 'Tollund man' found, preserved by mud, in Denmark in 1956.

▽ Alvan Marston had long held the notion of Piltdown man to be an error but argued that previous experts had made a genuine mistake and not fallen for a hoax.

△ 1954 saw the unearthing near
the official residence of London's
Lord Mayor, of a temple to Mithras, a
god of courage much worshipped by
Roman soldiers. The bull was a
sacrificial animal, whose blood
symbolized renewal of life.

◁ Michael Ventris deciphering
Linear B. The young British scholar
recognized the script as an early form
of Greek and was able to translate
thousands of clay tablets from the
Mycenaean period (1400–1000
B.C.) of Bronze Age Greece.

23

Building for the future

In the Western world, war prevented major building projects in the early 1940s. The main task was the reconstruction of basic facilities. The 1950s saw a renewal of interest in more ambitious schemes. The high priest of modern design was Charles-Édouard Jeanneret better known as Le Corbusier. His followers applauded his buildings as clean, simple and uncluttered. Critics called them cold, impossible to live in, even ugly.

In their view his 'international' style was simply filling the skyline of the world's great cities with filing cabinets. As if to reassert their own established reputations the leading architects of the previous generation produced outstanding new buildings—Mies van der Rohe's Seagram Building and Frank Lloyd Wright's Guggenheim Museum.

But most people had more practical concerns. Millions of Americans were moving to the suburbs where real estate developers had subdivided large tracts of land into residential areas, with several basic house designs repeated over and over. The picture window, the attached garage, and the backyard barbeque were standard to most designs. More than one homeowner suffered the embarrassing experience of driving up one street and down the next, trying to locate his own house in an ocean of houses that all looked alike.

◁ Brasilia – Brazil's new capital in the interior. The futuristic buildings and bold bow-and-arrow plan suggested a nation's self-confident thrust towards greatness.

△ The headquarters of the United Nations opened in 1951. In theory designed by a committee, it was based on the inspiration of one member – Le Corbusier.

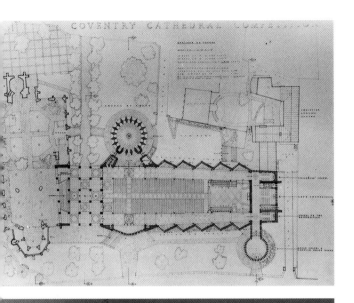

◁ Coventry Cathedral –
a symbol of Britain's post-
war recovery, blending
old and new. Sir Basil
Spence's competition
designs, submitted in
1951, incorporated the
shell of its bombed-out
Gothic predecessor.

▽ Levittown, a model
community designed by
Abraham Levitt for war
veterans, tried to
combine the green of the
small town and the
conveniences of the big
city.

◁ Le Corbusier's most
famous saying – "A
house is a machine for
living in" put him firmly
in the camp of the
'functionalists'. His own
designs – the chapel at
Ronchamp, the Indian
city of Chandigarh, large-
scale housing at
Marseilles – in the long
run mattered less than
his enormous influence
on the professions of
architecture and
planning.

Art and design

According to Sir Hugh Casson, design mastermind of the "Festival of Britain", the chaotic "taste" of the 1950s was an understandable reaction against the drab 1940s – "After ten years of austerity . . . people wanted the sensation of plenty . . . The result was . . . a binge of far too many colors and textures and changes of surface . . . It was like going into a sweet shop after being on a starvation diet."

In the visual arts, similar confusion seemed to reign on both sides of the Atlantic, with a widening gulf between the professional artist and the ordinary public. At the same time that paint-by-number kits were selling by the millions, New York's abstract expressionism school of painting was beginning to exert a major impact on the world of art.

Led by such innovators as Jackson Pollock and Willem de Kooning, this new approach would radically alter the direction of modern painting.

▽ Cecil Beaton's photographic model with a creation of "action painter" Jackson Pollock, who said "When I am painting I have no knowledge of what I am doing." Most people believed him.

△ British Sculptor Henry Moore with a terra cotta "Seated Figure" bearing an unusually striking resemblance to what one might expect such a subject to be.

△ Graham Sutherland's portrait of Churchill, commissioned by Parliament to mark the great man's 80th birthday was dismissed by its subject as 'a remarkable work of modern art' and later destroyed on his orders.

(Top right) The 'Ideal Home' of the 1950s favored the open plan concept, doing away with internal walls where possible to create a sense of greater space and light.

(Center right) Wallpapers, carpets and curtains with bold geometric designs in primary colors were seen as a revolt against the drab 'utility' patterns of war.

▷ Furniture of the 1950s favored spindly legs and plastic or 'textured' coverings. The brand names Ercol and G-Plan became synonymous with modern decor.

Popular music

The 1950s saw popular music begin its transition into 'pop'. In 1950 the crooner, backed by a big band, and the lavishly costumed stage musical, still reigned supreme. By the end of the decade however they had lost their young audiences to their new rivals – rock 'n' roll, jazz and, in Britain, skiffle, a sort of do-it-yourself country music played on homemade instruments, like the washboard and tea-chest double bass.

In 1950, Frank Sinatra was seen to replace Bing Crosby as America's highest-paid singer. "You can hear every word he sings – which is sometimes a pity" – remarked one critic but his London debut was still a sell-out. 1951 saw success on both sides of the Atlantic for *Kiss Me Kate* and *South Pacific*.

The decade closed with the death of jazz singer Billie Holiday at the age of 44. The development of higher quality recording techniques ('hi-fi') would ensure that generations yet unborn would be able to recapture the magic of her voice.

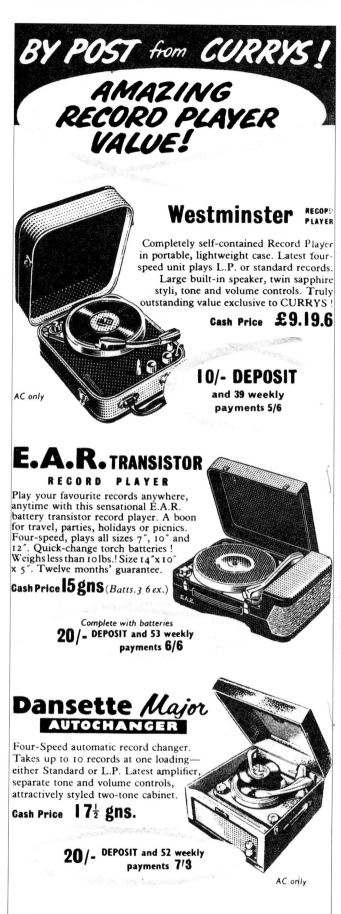

PEOPLE WILL SAY WE'RE IN LOVE

The THEATRE GUILD *presents at The* THEATRE ROYAL, *Drury Lane.*

OKLAHOMA!

(Based on the play "GREEN GROW THE LILACS" by Lynn Riggs)

Music by
RICHARD RODGERS
Book and Lyrics by
OSCAR HAMMERSTEIN 2ND

SONGS FROM THE SHOW
PEOPLE WILL SAY WE'RE IN LOVE • THE SURREY WITH THE FRINGE ON TOP
OUT OF MY DREAMS • OH, WHAT A BEAUTIFUL MORNIN'
I CAIN'T SAY NO • OKLAHOMA
PRICE 2/- EACH, NET

WILLIAMSON
MUSIC INC., NEW YORK.
CHAPPELL & CO LTD
PIANO SELECTION 3/- NET. • VOCAL SCORE 12/6 NET.

◁ Songs from American musicals like *Oklahoma, South Pacific* and *Carousel* became "standards," appealing to all ages.

△ Lightweight record players could transform a school hall into a dance hall or bring the stars to your own room.

▷ The slowly-revolving ($33\frac{1}{3}$ revolutions per minute) "long player," pressed in lightweight vinyl, offered an average of 20–25 minutes uninterrupted music per side – six tunes or a couple of movements of a symphony. Stacked ten high on a record-player this meant music for an entire evening. The LP's reign was to last for over thirty years until it was displaced by the even more portable cassette and compact disk.

△ Frank Sinatra performing at a 1952 concert in New York. He was voted the singer who had done most to raise popular taste in music.

▷ *The Boyfriend* by Sandy Wilson – a 1953 musical set in the 1920s, was staged in England to huge success. The 29-year-old composer spent the rest of his career re-staging it worldwide.

Rock and roll

One, two, three o'clock, four o'clock rock!
Five, six, seven o'clock, eight o'clock rock!
Nine, ten, eleven o'clock, twelve o'clock rock!
We're gonna rock around the clock tonight
Rock, rock, rock till broad daylight
We're gonna rock, rock, rock around the clock,
tonight!

The film was *Blackboard Jungle* and the band was Bill Haley and the Comets. In 1955, "Rock Around the Clock" stayed at the top of the charts for five months. In 1956 it became the title of a film about the new dance and music craze – rock 'n' roll. Britain's own stars had names hinting at impatience and violence – Marty Wilde, Billy Fury and Vince Eager. America kept in the headlines when three stars – Buddy Holly, Richie Valens and "Big Bopper," J. P. Richardson, died in a plane crash in 1959. For many, rock 'n' roll was a way of saying goodbye to childhood and no to being grown-up.

△ Johnny Ray serenades fans under his dressing-room window in Dublin. Like Sinatra, he had the knack of singing close to the microphone as though the only people present were him and each single member of the audience. His appeal was heightened by his well-publicized deafness.

△ Bill Haley and the Comets traded ballads for beat and sold 22,000,000 records in two years before new stars made them look old and old-fashioned.

▷ Cliff Richard in *Espresso Bongo*, a film satirizing the rise of a talentless pop star. The grand old man of British pop was still having the last laugh 30 years later.

◁ British star, Tommy Steele, (once Tommy Hicks) impresses young fans at his family home in south London's Bermondsey.

◁ Elvis Presley made a record for his mother's birthday in 1953. Three years later he was on TV at $50,000 a time and seeing his first hit record, "Heartbreak Hotel," sell 3,000,000 copies. In the next two years he earned $100,000,000. In 1958 he began two years military service as a GI in Germany.

▽ The great thing about rock 'n' roll dancing was that there were no set steps to learn. As Bill Haley said, "Its appeal is its simplicity. Everyone wants to get into the act. With rock 'n' roll they can join in."

Film and theater

In the 1950s most people still thought of films in terms of Hollywood and stars and as a form of entertainment. Intellectuals, who saw films as "art," raved about directors – from France (Tati, Truffaut), Italy (Fellini, De Sica), Sweden (Bergman) and even India (Satyajit Ray). Both types of film-goer, however, were gripped by the cult surrounding the magnetic James Dean. This charismatic actor starred in only three films before being tragically killed in a car crash at the age of 24.

England contributed the biggest hit of the decade in Lerner and Loewe's *My Fair Lady*, adapted from George Bernard Shaw's *Pygmalion*, and which starred Rex Harrison and Julie Andrews.

Two other big hits were *Bye, Bye Birdie*, a musical spoof of the Elvis Presley mania, and *West Side Story*, Leonard Bernstein's Broadway musical adaptation of *Romeo and Juliet*, starring Carol Lawrence and Larry Kert in 1957, later starring Natalie Wood in the movie version, set in a New York City slum and concerning rival teenage gangs.

△ In 1952, Cinerama used combat-simulation technology for pilots to produce a "wide-screen" effect, overwhelming audiences with the sense of "being there."

▽ Hollywood reclaimed its old superiority in the 1950's with lavish epics like *Ben Hur*. This film spectacular starring Charlton Heston was released in 1959.

◁ *Rebel without a Cause*, released in 1955, became the symbol of a generation of angry, disillusioned youth, and elevated James Dean to legend status. In the movie, Dean plays the part of a sensitive young man who is in revolt against a conformist society. In real life, Dean and his co-stars Natalie Wood and Sal Mineo later met violent ends – Dean in an auto crash, Wood in a drowning accident, and Mineo a murder victim.

▽ *A Streetcar Named Desire* (1951) not only launched Marlon Brando as a star name but also established his "scratch and mumble" style of super-realistic acting as the model for later youth heroes such as James Dean and Paul Newman.

▽ *Some Like It Hot*, starring Marilyn Monroe and Jack Lemmon, was a slick comedy classic that long out-lasted the decade in popular appeal. By 1957 "MM" was married to playwright Arthur Miller and playing opposite Laurence Olivier.

Growing up

The war years of the 1940's brought home to every nation the obvious truth that its children were its future. With a "baby boom" underway in the United States, many new parents turned for child-rearing guidance to best-seller *Baby and Child Care*, by Dr. Benjamin Spock.

Another influence upon parents and children was to be found in more and more living rooms across the nation. By 1955, over 50 million homes were equipped with TV sets, and America's first television generation formed the habit of passing many after-school hours being entertained by their favorite "boob tube" programs.

The Lone Ranger and *Hopalong Cassidy* were popular TV stars, as well as an endearing collie dog named *Lassie*. Young viewers joined the Mouseketeers in singing the Mickey Mouse show theme song: "M-i-c-k-e-y—M-o-u-s-e." Children were to encounter many more Disney characters directly when Disneyland opened in California in 1955.

△ The 1950s were filled with new experiences that were a by-product of changing lifestyles. Rising car-ownership, for example, made people better-traveled than ever before.

▷ Gang wars were representative of the aggression of youth. In big-city slums, gangs, fought in defense of "turf." Switch blades were usually the weapon of choice.

◁ The hula-hoop was so called because it needed a gyration of the hips like a Hawaiian hula dancer to keep it going. Promoted as fun for all ages it was funniest for manufacturers who made them for pennies to sell for dollars.

◁ For those teens with a drivers license and car, the drive-in hamburger stand was the place to see and be seen.

△ "Hand jive" gave youngsters a way to join in with music where it was too crowded to dance.

Fashion

Generally speaking only two social groups cared much about fashion in the 1950s – the well-off, who were the traditional market for Paris-based designers, and the working young generation, a new and rapidly-growing mass-market.

Middle class girls still dressed to look like their mothers, who dressed as though they were still in the 1930s, wearing hats, gloves and pearls on every conceivable occasion.

Young working people, however, looked to America, mirrored through the cinema and magazines, for their inspiration and imported blue jeans, check shirts, sloppy sweaters and suede shoes. In 1955 Mary Quant opened 'Bazaar' in the King's Road, London to sell simple clothes in casual styles. Henceforth fashion history would run in reverse with the old and rich imitating their younger social inferiors.

△ 'Teddy Boys' got their name from the echo of the Edwardian era suggested by their flamboyant dress. In fact the American river-boat gambler, with his 'string' tie, draped jacket and gaudy waistcoat was a more likely model.

◁ In the 1950s Americans rediscovered jeans, the tough blue denim work-trousers originally invented for the western cow-hand. The craze reached Britain in 1955, but were seen at first as only being a woman's garment.

△ "Bermudas" – inspired by the tropical uniform of the British Colony's military band seen by tourists.

△ The simple floral print cotton summer dress retained its popularity throughout the 1950s, despite the occasional efforts of British fashion manufacturers to imitate the more extreme styles of Parisian haute couture.

▷ Only working-class young men were drawn to the eye-catching Teddy Boy style. Other males remained traditional and wore hats to cover slicked-back hair. The cut-down duffle coat hints at memories of wartime service in the navy.

Sports

Better communications, both through jet flights and the spread of television, gave sports an increasingly international character throughout the decade. The 1952 (Helsinki) and 1956 (Melbourne) Olympics provided grand set-piece contests. In Helsinki, Czech Emil Zatopek won the 10,000 meters and 5,000 meters and then entered his first-ever marathon to win that as well. In Melbourne, Australia's women swimmers and athletes stole the show.

There were other shocks, too. In 1950, England entered soccer's World Cup for the first time only to be knocked out 1–0 by an amateur American side. England returned the compliment in 1951 when the unknown Randolph Turpin defeated Sugar Ray Robinson for the middleweight world title. Record-breakers of the decade included American Florence Chadwick, who in 1950 swam the English Channel in 13 hours 28 minutes; Yankee baseball player Mickey Mantle, who set many World Series records; England's Donald Campbell, who set a new world water-speed record of 202 mph in 1955; and 21 year old Garfield Sobers of the West Indies who set a new record Test cricket score in 1958, hammering 365 off Pakistan – not out. In the same year, Australian Herb Elliott set new world records in both the mile and 1500 meters.

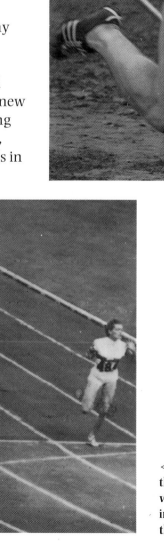

△ On May 6, 1954 Roger Bannister became the first man to run a mile in under four minutes.

◁ Betty Cuthbert, star of the Australian team, winning the 100 meters in Melbourne. She won the 200 meters as well.

(Far left) In November 1953, Hungary defeated England 6–3. The visitors' superior skills brought a new respect for "continental" style soccer with its emphasis on ball skills rather than physical contact.

Forward Bobby Charlton was one of the lucky survivors of the tragic Munich air crash in 1958 which killed seven of his Manchester United team mates.

(Below left) In 1951 Maureen "Little Mo" Connolly became, at 16, the youngest-ever winner of the U.S. tennis championships.

▽ In 1951, Rocky Marciano (right) – world heavyweight champion (1952–56) – knocked former champion Joe Louis out of the ring.

On the move

Sales of automobiles between 1945 and 1955 tripled in the United States as industry shifted from manufacturing war material to consumer goods. Coupled with this was a massive building program of highways that crisscrossed the country, enabling millions of Americans to move out of the cities and into newly created suburbs. In effect, people's lives came to revolve around the automobile.

Other means of getting from one place to another also improved. In 1951, a British Canberra jet bomber set a new 4 hour 40 minutes record for crossing the Atlantic, and 1958 saw BOAC introduce the world's first scheduled transatlantic air service.

Americans were slow to make the transfer from train to plane. By 1955, a national survey revealed that only 25 percent had ever flown; seven years later the number had increased to 36 percent.

For young rebels, the motorcycle represented rebellion and freedom. Members of motorcycle clubs, wearing standard garb of black leather jackets and boots, traveled the highways in search of their own American dream.

△ In 1959, Britain's *Flying Saucer*, the Saunders Roe "Hovercraft," made history on the 50th anniversary of Louis Bleriot's flight across the Channel by crossing from Calais to Dover in 2 hours 3 minutes on its 10 inch cushion of air. Bleriot had done it in 43 minutes.

◁ A drive-in movie at Barajas, outside Madrid. Unpredictable weather conditions in Europe, and the lower average level of car-ownership, meant that the drive-in remained largely an American phenomenon.

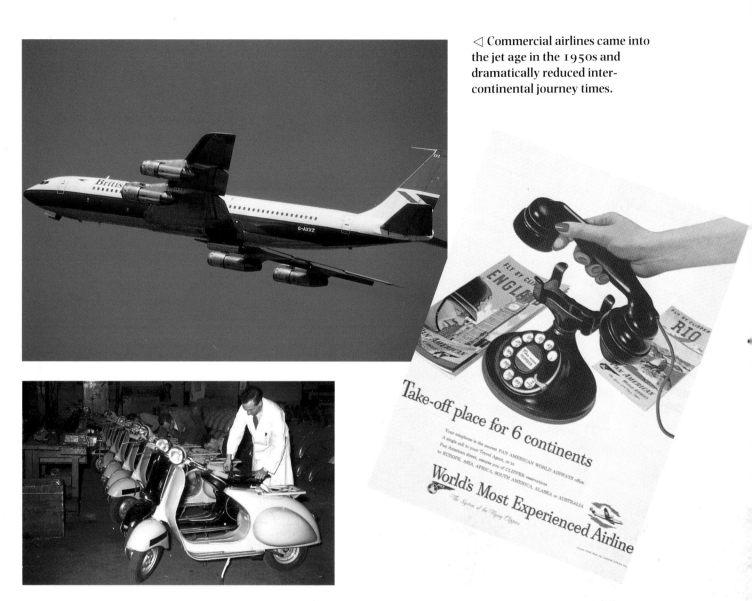

◁ Commercial airlines came into the jet age in the 1950s and dramatically reduced inter-continental journey times.

△ Nippy Vespa and Lambretta motor scooters from Italy offered a new rival to the traditional motorbike. Their sleek styling was attractive and hire-purchase payment schemes put them within reach of the teenager.

▷ The car of choice for many families living in the suburbs was the station wagon. Not only was there room for the family. but also groceries and even the family dog!

Science and medicine

The launching of the Russian satellite *Sputnik* in October 1957 stunned the United States and marked the beginning of a "space race" between the superpowers. A month later, "space dog" Laika became the first living creature to orbit the earth. In 1958, American Explorer satellites revealed for the first time the existence of belts of radiation around the earth. They were named in honor of James Van Allen, their discoverer. Medicine saw numerous "firsts" in the course of the decade – kidney transplant, artificial hearts used in surgery, inserted heart pacemakers, an oral contraceptive pill and sex-change operations. Less happily it also saw the first widespread use of the drug Thalidomide which was to deform thousands of babies. Practical technological advances included direct telephone dialing, Xerox machines, fan heaters, nonstick pans, new artificial textiles like Orlon, and transistor radios.

▷ In March 1953, Dr. Jonas E. Salk announced success in tests of his new vaccine against the child killer-disease, polio – 'infantile paralysis.' In 1954, in the first mass-vaccination 1,829,916 Michigan children were immunized.

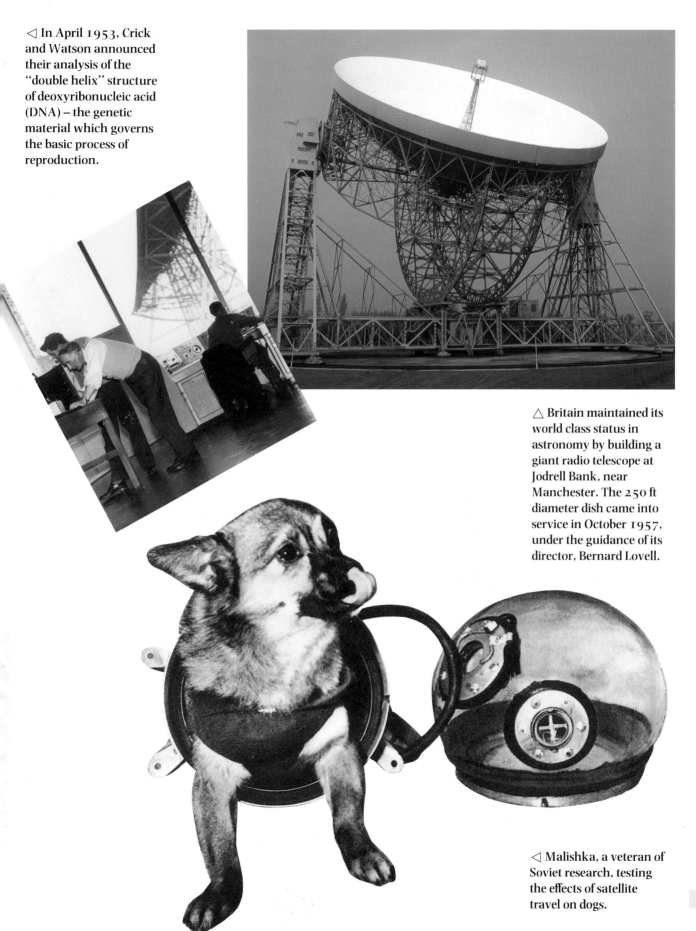

◁ In April 1953, Crick and Watson announced their analysis of the "double helix" structure of deoxyribonucleic acid (DNA) – the genetic material which governs the basic process of reproduction.

△ Britain maintained its world class status in astronomy by building a giant radio telescope at Jodrell Bank, near Manchester. The 250 ft diameter dish came into service in October 1957, under the guidance of its director, Bernard Lovell.

◁ Malishka, a veteran of Soviet research, testing the effects of satellite travel on dogs.

43

Personalities of the 1950s

Adenauer, Konrad (1876–1967), former mayor of Cologne who became the first Chancellor of the Federal Republic of Germany (1949–63).

Bernstein, Leonard (1918–), American conductor who composed the music for *West Side Story* (1957).

Bogart, Humphrey (1899–1957), American film star, renowned for "tough guy" roles as in *The African Queen* (1951).

Bohr, Niels (1885–1962), Danish scientist who organised the first "Atoms for Peace" conference in 1955.

Britten, Benjamin (1913–76), British composer, famed for operas like *Billy Budd* (1951) and *Gloriana* (1953).

Burgess, Guy (1911–63), British diplomat who, with Donald Maclean (1913–), revealed himself as a double agent by defecting to the Soviet Union in 1951. He lived out the rest of his life in exile.

Chaplin, Charlie (1889–1977), British film actor who left the United States for Swiss exile during the McCarthy era. He wrote, directed and starred in the film *Limelight* (1953), the masterpiece of his later career. He also composed its hit theme tune.

Dulles, John Foster (1888–1959), American Secretary of State (1953–9) noted for his unyielding anti-communism and willingness to play at "brinkmanship" in international confrontations.

Einstein, Albert (1879–1955), German-born American scientist whose work in theoretical physics won him the Nobel Prize and made possible the development of atomic weapons. He was himself a passionate supporter of nuclear disarmament and said of his own achievements "If only I had known I should have become a watchmaker."

Golding, William (1911–), British author best known for *Lord of the Flies* (1954) which suggested how thin was modern man's veneer of civilization.

Guinness, Sir Alec (1914–), British film actor, star of *The Bridge on the River Kwai*, knighted in 1959.

Hemingway, Ernest (1899–1961), American adventurer and author of the semiautobiographical *The Old Man and the Sea* (1952). Winner of the Nobel Prize for Literature 1954.

Kefauver, Estes (1903–1963), U.S. senator from Tennessee, who, during the early fifties, headed a special committee to investigate crime, the hearings of which were televised

nationwide and watched by millions of fascinated Americans.

Kelly, Gene (1912–), American singer/dancer/actor best known for *Singin' in the Rain* (1952)

Kelly, Grace (1929–82), American film actress and star of *High Society* (1956) who joined it by marrying Prince Rainier III of Monaco.

Kenyatta, Jomo (1893–1978), African nationalist leader, imprisoned 1953–60 for alleged leadership of the "Mau Mau" rebellion, which he always denied. He became the first Prime Minister of an independent Kenya (1963) and later its president until his death.

Khrushchev, Nikita (1894–1971), First Secretary of the Soviet Communist Party from 1953 and Prime Minister of the Soviet Union 1958–64. He "destalinized" Russia by governing without terror but crushed risings in satellite countries. He improved relations with the West but worsened them with China. Failure of his economic policies drove him from power.

King, Jr., Martin Luther (1929–68), American baptist minister and leader of the civil rights movement. He received the Nobel Peace Prize in 1964.

Jomo Kenyatta

Nikita Khrushchev

Martin Luther King Jnr.

Loewe, Frederick (1901–), American composer of hit musicals *My Fair Lady* (1956) and *Gigi* (1958).

Macmillan, Harold (1894–1986), British Conservative politician who dominated the 1950s as Minister of Housing, Chancellor of the Exchequer and Prime Minister (1957–63). His chief international success was a nuclear "test ban treaty" but he failed to get Britain into the European Economic Community.

Margaret, Princess (1930–), public disapproval in 1955 made it impossible for her to marry divorced Group Captain Peter Townsend. In 1960 she married photographer Anthony Armstrong-Jones.

McCarthy, Joseph (1908–57), U.S. senator from Wisconsin who led a witch hunt for suspected communists in government.

Menzies, Sir Robert (1894–1978), veteran Australian politician, Prime Minister 1949–66. He favored close links with the United Kingdom.

Monroe, Marilyn (1926–62), Hollywood actress who, because of her voluptuous good looks and sultry manner, was called the "sex symbol."

Nagy, Imre (1895–1958), lifelong Hungarian communist who, as Prime Minister after the 1956 rising, promised free elections. He was overthrown by Soviet invaders, tried and shot.

Nehru, Jawaharlal (1889–1964), first Prime Minister of independent India (1947–64). He stood for industrial modernization and social reform.

Orwell, George (1903–50), real name Eric Blair, British writer and socialist whose prophetic novel *Nineteen Eighty-four* (1949) warned of the dangers of totalitarian rule.

Pasternak, Boris (1890–1960), Russian poet and author of *Doctor Zhivago*. Winner of the Nobel Prize for Literature in 1958, which he was not allowed to collect as his writing was considered too critical of the Soviet state.

Pearson, Lester (1897–1972), Canadian diplomat, who served as President of the UN General Assembly (1952–3) and won the Nobel Peace Prize in 1957.

Presley, Elvis Aaron (1935–77), American singer and actor. Accused by critics of "sneering with his legs," he won the nickname "Elvis the Pelvis," before outstripping all rivals to become "the King." Served as a private in the US army in Germany 1958–9.

Schweitzer, Albert (1875–1965), medical missionary and talented organist whose work among African lepers won him the Nobel Peace Prize in 1952.

Stevenson, Adlai (1900–65), American statesman and unsuccessful presidential candidate in 1952 and 1956.

Thomas, Dylan (1914–53), Welsh poet chiefly remembered for his radio verse drama *Under Milk Wood*, read by rising young actor Richard Burton in a posthumous production in 1954.

Joseph McCarthy

Elvis Presley

Albert Schweitzer

1950s year by year

1950

- Alger Hiss convicted in America for perjury in concealing Communist party membership.
- Senator McCarthy alleges State Department employs over 200 Communists.
- Fuchs imprisoned for betraying British atom secrets to the Soviet Union.
- Russia announces it has an atom bomb.
- End of gasoline rationing in Britain.
- Outbreak of war in Korea leads to involvement of UN and Chinese forces.
- Uruguay wins the World Cup.
- Diners Club issues first credit cards.
- Death of George Bernard Shaw.
- President Truman authorizes production of H-bomb.
- U.S. sends 35 military advisers to South Vietnam.

1951

- President Truman dismisses General MacArthur as Far East commander.
- Prime Minister Mossadeq nationalizes the oil industry in Iran.
- British spies Burgess and Maclean defect to the Soviet Union.
- Conservative government replaces Labor in Britain.
- Libya becomes an independent state.
- First Miss World contest staged.
- J. D. Salinger publishes cult novel *The Catcher in the Rye*.
- Death of William Randolph Hearst, eccentric American newspaper tycoon.
- First commercial manufacture of electronic computers.

1952

- Death of King George VI, succession of Queen Elizabeth II.
- Eisenhower wins landslide victory in U.S. Presidential election.
- Army coup in Egypt overthrows King Farouk.
- Britain tests atomic bomb.
- 'Mau Mau' movement leads to state of emergency in Kenya.
- Death of Eva Peron, wife of dictator of Argentina.
- United States explodes an H-bomb.
- World's first jet airline service (London-Johannesberg).
- 'Cinerama' wide-screen movies first exhibited.
- First transistorized hearing aid.
- First teabags marketed in Britain.
- Agatha Christie's mystery play *The Mousetrap* begins nonstop run.
- Olympic Games held in Helsinki.
- Peace agreement between West Germany, United States, Britain and France signed.
- "I Love Lucy" starring Lucille Ball, makes its TV debut.

1953

- Death of Stalin.
- Coronation of Queen Elizabeth II.
- Hillary and Tenzing conquer Everest.
- Soviet troops crush workers' rising in East Berlin.
- Armistice ends fighting in Korea.
- Military coup in Iran overthrows Mossadeq and reinstates the Shah.
- John F. Kennedy marries Jacqueline Bouvier.
- Winston Churchill wins Nobel Prize for Literature.
- Russians explode an H-bomb in Siberia.
- Ian Fleming publishes first James Bond book *Casino Royale*.
- First music synthesizer.
- First car with fiberglass body – the Chevrolet Corvette.

1954

- French army defeated at Dien Bien Phu by Vietnamese.
- Billy Graham crusades in America and Britain.
- Medical research confirms link between smoking and cancer.
- Fall of Senator McCarthy after condemnation by U.S. Senate.
- Japanese crew of fishing boat *Lucky Dragon* contaminated by radioactive fall-out from U.S. H-bomb test at Bikini Atoll.
- Nasser emerges as Egypt's leader.
- Pope launches Eurovision TV network.
- West Germany wins soccer World Cup.
- Roger Bannister runs world's first sub four minute mile.
- Algerian nationalists begin rising against French rule.
- J. R. R. Tolkien publishes *Lord of the Rings*.
- *Nautilus* launched as world's first nuclear submarine.
- Racial segregation in public schools is ruled unconstitutional by U.S. Supreme Court.
- Southeast Asia Treaty Organization (SEATO) formed by U.S., Britain, Australia, New Zealand, Philippines, Pakistan, and Thailand.

1955

- Churchill replaced by Eden as Prime Minister.
- Warsaw Pact established as Russian-led military alliance.
- Argentine dictator Peron overthrown.
- European Parliament holds first meeting at Strasbourg.
- Commercial television (ITV) begins in Britain.
- Bus boycott by blacks begins in segregated Montgomery, Alabama.
- Wave of 'Flying Saucer' sightings reported.

● Fiber optics developed at Imperial College, London.
● High-speed dental drill introduced in Sweden.
● Best selling record of the year is "Rock Around the Clock," by Bill Haley and the Comets.

1956

● Khrushchev denounces Stalin's terror.
● Anti-Soviet risings in Poland and Hungary crushed.
● Nasser nationalizes Suez Canal – Britain and France withdraw from abortive invasion of Egypt after disapproval of the United States but Israelis seize Sinai.
● Re-election of Eisenhower as U.S. President.
● Transatlantic telephone service begins.
● Fairey Delta fighter sets air speed record of 1132 mph.
● First video recorder manufactured.
● First Go-Kart built.
● Abstract expressionist painter, Jackson Pollock, killed in automobile accident.
● America's two largest labor unions merge to become the AFL-CIO.

1957

● Treaty of Rome establishes European Economic Community.
● Republic of Ireland declares state of emergency to fight the IRA.
● Malaya becomes independent.
● Russia launches *Sputnik I*, the world's first space satellite.
● Death of French designer Christian Dior.
● Gold Coast becomes independent as Ghana.
● Britain tests its own H-bomb.
● Building of Brazil's new capital at Brasilia begins.
● Jodrell Bank radio telescope completed.

● Sony market first pocket-sized transistor radio.
● Soviet Union launches first Intercontinental Ballistic Missile.
● Frisbee invented.
● U.S. Congress approves first civil rights bill for blacks since Reconstruction.
● President Eisenhower sends federal troops to Little Rock, Arkansas, to enforce desegregation of the public schools.
● "Beat" novel *On the Road*, by Jack Kerouac.

1958

● Campaign for Nuclear Disarmament (CND) launched in Britain.
● De Gaulle returns to power in France to deal with crisis in Algeria.
● Chinese crush national rising in Tibet.
● John XXIII becomes Pope.
● U.S. forces land in "peace-keeping" operation in Lebanon.
● First stereo records marketed.
● Integrated circuit (microchip) invented.
● *Explorer I*, first U.S. satellite to go into orbit, is launched from Cape Canaveral.
● First domestic jet airline passenger service in United States begins.
● Boris Pasternak's *Doctor Zhivago* is top-selling novel of the year.

1959

● Fidel Castro seizes power in Cuba.
● De Gaulle becomes President of the Fifth French Republic.
● Death of American architect Frank Lloyd Wright.
● NASA picks first astronaut team.
● First U.S. ballistic-missile, *George Washington*, launched at Groton, Connecticut.
● Soviet satellite *Lunik III* sends back

first photographs of the far side of the moon.
● European Free Trade Association (EFTA) set up by UK, Austria, Portugal, Switzerland, Sweden, Norway and Denmark.
● Archbishop Makarios becomes first President of the independent Republic of Cyprus.
● Alaska becomes 49th state of the United States.
● Singapore becomes independent.
● Hawaii becomes 50th state of the United States.
● St. Lawrence Seaway opens.
● First transatlantic TV transmission.
● Soviet Premier Khrushchev visits United States, making transcontinental tour.

Index